THE A-Z OF INEQUALITY

THE A-Z OF INEQUALITY

SEBASTIAN CHAMBERS

Illustrated by Helena Maxwell

*For my wonderful family
who have had to put up with me
discussing these ideas for far too long*

CONTENTS

Foreword	xi
Introduction	1
Avoidance of tax	9
Bank bailouts	11
Capital gains tax	13
Debt and interest	15
Entrepreneurs' and Business Investment Relief	17
Farm subsidies	19
Green taxes and subsidies	21
Housing and other stamp duty	23
Inflation	25
Jail is for the little people	27
Kicking the can down the road	29
Lifetime ISAs	31
Marginal rates of income tax	33
National Insurance	35

Offshore tax havens	37
Planning regulation	39
Quantitative easing	41
Rates and council tax	43
Self-Invested Personal Pensions (SIPPs)	45
Trusts and inheritance tax	47
Unpaid wages	49
VAT	51
Women and wealth	53
X marks the spot of hidden treasure	55
Young people	57
Zero Interest Rate Policy (ZIRP)	59
Conclusion	61

Sebastian Chambers (Author)

Sebastian Chambers has first-hand experience of the practices and policies covered in *The A-Z of Inequality*, having had over thirty years' experience in the City advising private equity, banks and debt funds. He is a non-executive director of CIL Management Consultants, Neptune (the home interiors business) and STL Tech (the innovation incubator). Sebastian is an active Angel investor and has backed a range of start-ups, including SupplyCompass, KeyNest and Slip Safety. Sebastian is Chair of Trustees for Firefly International, a Scottish charity that works with children impacted by conflict in Bosnia and the Middle East. Prior to 2020, he was a partner at CIL for over twenty years, working with high-growth UK and US companies and the private equity investors that back them. Previously, he ran a factory making doors and building panels. Sebastian is a chartered accountant, spending five years with PwC – where he was an audit manager for clients including Bank of America and BNP Paribas. He has a degree in economics and social sciences from Manchester University.

Helena Maxwell (Illustrator)

Helena is an artist, illustrator and teacher. She works with a broad range of publishers and has a regular slot in the *Sunday Times* money section. She studied fine art at Bath College and the Royal Drawing School and has a degree in English literature from King's College, London.

Laurens McDonald (Researcher)

Laurens specialises in social science research using quantitative, qualitative and interdisciplinary techniques. He read philosophy, politics and economics at Oxford University and has a master's in global political economy from Bristol University.

FOREWORD

We live in the most prosperous time in human history; there are fewer people in poverty than ever before. Modern smartphones connect us and provide limitless entertainment. We are on the verge of benefitting from a wide array of revolutionary technologies, from cancer-busting drugs to flying cars. Yet all does not feel right. There's a nagging sensation among many that there is injustice being perpetrated.

The British Social Attitudes survey found in 2020 that almost two-thirds (65%) of people in England think that the income distribution is 'unfair'. These people are more likely to engage in politics to express their discomfort. An Ipsos MORI poll at the end of 2020 found that two-thirds (65%) believe that the UK is in decline and a majority (57%) believe that today's children will have a worse life than their parents.

They may not be entirely wrong. The United Kingdom experienced an economically stagnant decade through the 2010s while the likes of Germany and the US steamed ahead. The forecasts indicate that there is little hope of faster growth over the coming decade after the Covid bounce back. Looking further ahead the challenges are mounting. There is an ageing population putting great demands on a declining number of working-age people for the likes of pensions, health and social care.

People are not necessarily being rewarded for their efforts. Even young people on a successful path – those who have gone to university – are left with a large amount of debt and questions about whether their education was worthwhile. Many are still living at home well into adulthood. Young people who arrive in cities, to get a jump forward in their careers, find themselves held back by exorbitant rent. Meanwhile, the dream of home ownership is slipping away.

In *The A-Z of Inequality*, entrepreneur, investor and adviser Sebastian Chambers takes a microscope to the systematic inequalities driving our malaise and frustrations. He highlights how the state has been captured by the most privileged, resulting in numerous hidden tricks that favour the most privileged. These issues are far too rarely discussed in day-to-day debate but are having real impacts and call for serious reform.

The range of issues that Chambers tackles is impressive, inspired by his time on the coalface of the business world. To start, the tax system is broken. It's far too complex, allowing the rich to manoeuvre to pay less. It's also badly targeted. We viciously tax people who work, including through National Insurance that is avoided by the wealthy, yet refuse to properly tax land and other wealth.

The spending side is not much better. Bank bailouts have encouraged risky behaviour. Farm subsidies give free money to wealthy landowners even when they damage the environment. Meanwhile, monetary manipulation creates inflation and erodes the value of savings.

Then there's the gigantic intergenerational unfairness. Young people shoulder the debt, don't get to own a home and face growing education costs. Government debt puts a huge burden on to future generations while the state refuses to acknowledge its full liabilities. Planning regulations restrict housing where people want to live, pushing up the cost of living. Stamp duty gums up the property market, discouraging downsizing and leading to fewer appropriate homes for young families.

In *The A-Z of Inequality*, Chambers brings together extensive research and life experience in an approachable and easy-to-understand manner supported by beautiful illustrations. It's something anyone can get their head around, perhaps even our politicians.

Matthew Lesh is the head of research at the Adam Smith Institute

INTRODUCTION

Generation rent is getting fed up with the boomers. We know something is going wrong with wealth inequality. The gap is widening between those that own houses, shares and other assets, versus those that don't. The more you own, the wider the gap.

This book is about 'wealth inequality' not 'income inequality'. Over the past hundred years, governments have had a track record of reducing income inequality; through taxes on income and the provision of benefits, as well as publicly funded health and education. Wealth inequality is a different matter. We have seen the prices of houses, shares and other assets rise inexorably. Fine if you are an owner. Not so fine if you are a renter, or someone wanting to buy a home, or invest in a company.

The downside of capitalism is that it can create extremes of inequality. The upside is that it generates innovation and wealth to alleviate many of society's challenges. Almost everyone recognises that government has a key role to play in spreading the benefit of this upside of a market economy. Almost nobody thinks it is government's role to exacerbate inequality. Yet in my experience, UK governments, of all political parties, do exactly this – create wealth inequality.

During the Great Financial Crisis of 2008-9, after the initial market shock, I started to notice the value of my house, land and shares rising. In 2020 Covid-19 gave us the deepest recession in 300 years and we witnessed the same thing. There I was, working from home, looking at the value of stuff I own soar. It is embarrassing. This can't be right – recessions are supposed to give the market economy a bit of a reset. The young, capable and prudent are supposed to get the chance to buy a home that has fallen in value or buy into a business. This didn't happen; the market economy isn't working.

I have long been aware of some rules and loopholes that seem to favour only those who already have assets. What I began to realise is that these government-created advantages for the wealthy are systemic. As I started to write down the unequal rules in taxation, fiscal and monetary policy, they formed themselves into an alphabet. Even difficult letters like Q and Z stood for Quantitative Easing and Zero Interest Rate Policy, which both sit at the heart of the malaise in our financial system.

Over the course of the past twenty years, I began to notice that when I went to work on a Monday, the burden of taxation on that work was rising. We now have total marginal rates of tax including employers' and employees' National Insurance on earned income in excess of 60 per cent. However, when I came home on a Friday evening, something magic happened. Free of the responsibilities of work, I could start to enjoy a house and garden that always seemed to go up in value, an ever-growing tax-free

ISA portfolio, tax-free pension savings, even subsidised farmland. I could benefit from cheap debt to buy more assets, and these protected me from inflation and enabled me to make capital gains. By the simple act of leaving work and going home, I moved from being a contributing member of society, to being someone the state apparently feels the need to support. This isn't capitalism. It is a travesty created by successive governments.

Some of what has gone wrong has probably happened by accident. The devaluation of our money started with the enormous cost of paying for the First World War and was then compounded by the Second World War. The introduction of tax breaks for pension saving and then ISAs was designed to give people more of a stake in the economy and encourage savings. In some cases, politicians and civil servants are just ignorant of how the rules they make work in practice. One of the reasons I needed to write this book is that I understand how the rules for the rich work.

Not all has happened by accident. Some of the advantages for the wealthy have been created by special interest groups representing companies, financiers and landowners. Politicians have tended to favour homeowners over renters; not least because owner-occupiers are more likely to vote. The house price crash in the early 1990s created a long shadow; there is no doubt that the Labour, then Coalition and now Conservative governments have worked to stop house prices correcting from their current unaffordable levels.

Those that are missing out are growing in number. There is a burgeoning sense of injustice. If we continue to stack the rules in favour of the rich, we are heading for disaster. Young people are carrying an ever-greater burden of:

- Low wages
- High taxation on work
- Unaffordable housing (either to buy or rent)
- The repayment of student loans
- An ever-growing burden of government debt
- An ageing population
- Climate change

Solving these challenges is, however, not as difficult as it may appear. In the A-Z we look at how the state causes inequality, why it is damaging and what can be done about it.

Note: The fact base in the A-Z, and suggested policy changes, have been painstakingly researched by Laurens McDonald and beautifully illustrated by Helena Maxwell. We have decided to keep the book short and accessible. If you would be interested in seeing the underlying research, please visit A-ZofInequality.com

THE A-Z OF INEQUALITY

Avoidance of tax

Bank bailouts

Capital gains tax

Debt and interest

Entrepreneurs' and Business Investment Relief

Farm subsidies

Green taxes and subsidies

Housing and other stamp duty

Inflation

Jail is for the little people

Kicking the can down the road

Lifetime ISAs

Marginal rates of income tax

National Insurance

Offshore tax havens

Planning regulation

Quantitative easing

Rates and council tax

Self-Invested Personal Pensions (SIPPs)

Trusts and inheritance tax

Unpaid wages

VAT

Women and wealth

X marks the spot of hidden treasure

Young people

Zero Interest Rate Policy (ZIRP)

AVOIDANCE OF TAX

Tax avoidance is the preserve of the wealthy

Most people don't have much choice about paying their taxes. Income tax and National Insurance are deducted under pay as you earn (PAYE). VAT and duty are paid when we buy things. Not much room for manoeuvre. This isn't the case for the wealthy – they have specialist advisors who help them legally reduce their tax bills. Choices are made as to the most tax-efficient way to take income. Wealth is put into trusts, offshore accounts and special purpose vehicles – whatever they are. There are hundreds of legal tricks of the trade.

Not paying up is expensive and toxic

Avoidance may be legal, but it costs billions in lost tax: £33 billion as estimated by the UK tax authorities. It goes against our sense of fair play. Do we want to continue to live in a society where there is one set of rules for the rich and another set for everyone else?

Simplification

The tax code should be rewritten from scratch and made short and simple. The current UK tax code runs to 17,000 pages – the vast majority of this is irrelevant to most people. The more rules, the more loopholes. We need tax simplification.

BANK BAILOUTS

The state bailed out private sector institutions

During the financial crisis of 2008-9, the UK government devoted substantial resources to bailing out failed banks, including non-UK banks. Current and future taxpayers underwrote the failure of private companies. The government decided to devote our resources to these institutions and their wealthy depositors, rather than other priorities such as housing, healthcare or reducing the tax burden on the young.

Moral hazard

Effectively, the profits of banks are private and result in reinvestment for future profit, as well as the payment of bonuses and dividends. However, when banks make substantial losses and run out of cash, the state steps in. For the bankers it is 'heads I win, tails you lose'.

Let the banks fend for themselves

If a bank goes bust, it should largely be left for the private sector to clear up. Depositors should be protected by insurance and rank ahead of other lenders in the event of a failure. Bonuses and dividends in the previous year should be forfeited. All stakeholders should be protected by the diligent oversight of the directors, the Bank of England and other regulators. If any financial institution is too big to fail - so large that its failure poses a substantial risk to our society - it should be broken up.

A-ZofInequality.com

CAPITAL GAINS TAX

An allowance for the rich

Capital gains arise when you buy something like shares or property and sell it for a profit. Each person can make over £12,000 worth of capital gains a year tax free. This capital gains tax allowance is worth almost exactly the same as the income tax free allowance; a rich person gets the same allowance for making a capital gain as a working person does on their income.

Bed and breakfast

The allowance can be used each year. It is possible to sell enough shares at the end of each year to use up the allowance and then buy shares back in the new tax year, a practice known as bed and breakfast. Over the course of a few years it is possible to protect hundreds of thousands of pounds' worth of property and shares from paying any capital gains tax.

People who make capital gains should pay tax

We are fortunate to live in a society where it is possible to make investments and later sell them at a profit. Those able to take advantage of this should make a contribution to the cost of the services that makes this sort of society possible. There is no justification for an allowance that only the wealthy can take advantage of. The capital gains tax allowance needs to go.

DEBT AND INTEREST

Company and rental property owners have a huge advantage

Most people pay interest on their mortgage and other loans after they have paid their tax. But not the rich – they reduce the amount of tax they pay by deducting the interest before tax. That is why it is cheaper for a company to buy a house than it is for a first-time buyer. Generation rent is no accident – it is caused by the rules set by government.

There is too much debt

The fact that interest is tax deductible and dividends aren't, means that companies use debt more than shares. We are at risk of a corporate debt bubble. If a quoted company raises money from shareholders – once a major function of the City – it is considered a failure; any company that could, would just borrow more. Moreover, because new money is created when debt is issued, this excessive debt can cause instability in the money supply and create inflation.

A single change that would transform society

Interest payments should no longer be deducted when calculating tax. This would level the playing field between incorporated landlords and people buying their own home. Companies would use shareholders more and lenders less. Finance providers would become more engaged with the businesses they back. Our monetary system would be more stable.

A-ZofInequality.com

ENTREPRENEURS' AND BUSINESS INVESTMENT RELIEF

Tax incentives for richer owners

Entrepreneurs' Relief and Business Investment Relief mean that owners often pay only 50 per cent of the capital gains tax that others pay when a business is sold. Entrepreneurs' Relief is worth £100,000; Investment Relief is worth ten times as much. Employee shareholders with a small percentage of shares aren't eligible – they pay the full amount of capital gains tax.

Wealth is created by work

Wealth is created by work. Entrepreneurship is not the preserve of the main owners of a business. Often innovation and successful risk-taking come from across the team. Capitalism is fantastic at encouraging productive work. The main downside of capitalism is that the proceeds of that work are not evenly distributed. There is no case for the government to incentivise major business owners ahead of smaller employee investors. In some cases, Entrepreneurs' and Investment Reliefs can encourage owners to sell a business when perhaps a more long-term investment perspective would be better.

Capital gains tax should apply to all equally

We should scrap both Entrepreneurs' and Investment Relief. This would mean employee shareholders are treated the same as major business owners when it comes to selling shares. Our system already has a relief for entrepreneurs and investors – it is called capitalism.

FARM SUBSIDIES

Farm subsidies

The era of farm subsidies has been marked by the widespread use of pesticides, herbicides and other environmentally damaging intensive production methods. While some subsidies are paid for environmentally sensitive schemes, is this really an area for state intervention? Farmers husbanded the land themselves for generations before these schemes were introduced. It is ridiculous that taxpayers hand over money to farmers to simultaneously damage and improve the environment.

Subsidies for the rich

Many people think that introducing a cap on benefits is reasonable; does anyone think that wealthy farmers should have uncapped benefits? Some large landowners receive directly, or indirectly via their rents, benefits in excess of £100,000. Moreover, farming businesses are not subject to inheritance tax and sometimes get windfalls from planning permission. It's amazing that government devotes so much resource to this cause.

End farm subsidies

All farming subsidies should be phased out completely within five years – as was successfully done in New Zealand. Poorer farmers on low incomes should be rightly protected by the benefits safety net. Wealthier farmers should fend for themselves.

GREEN TAXES AND SUBSIDIES

Government has a critical role in tackling climate change

Consumers, companies, governments and international bodies all have a vital role to play in tackling the causes of climate change. Taxes, subsidies and planning permission for renewables are the core policy tools for government in what may be the defining challenge of our era.

Some policies have benefitted the wealthy

Landowners and other wealthy investors have received huge subsidies for onshore wind and solar farms. These subsidies are paid for by supplements on home utility bills - a straight transfer of cash from ordinary people to the wealthy. A renewable heat incentive scheme in Northern Ireland was so abused by landowners that it led to the collapse of Northern Ireland's devolved government - a major blow to the peace process, as well as to public support for green policies.

Green policy should not subsidise the wealthy

Over the coming years we are going to need a massive focus on environmental policy, as well as on our personal and corporate behaviours. Might it be useful to screen policy and behaviours for who benefits and who pays? We all need to buy into positive environmental change; a fairer system is likely to be more sustainable in all senses.

HOUSING AND OTHER STAMP DUTY

Stamp duty stops mobility

Free markets are generally good at matching buyers and sellers, but stamp duty – a tax on the buying and selling of property and shares – is stopping markets functioning properly. The elderly often feel trapped in what was their family home, as the cost of downsizing can be prohibitive – largely because of stamp duty. This restricts the number of homes available for younger families.

Guess who can get out of stamp duty?

The very wealthy don't need to sell property – even if it is left empty – and therefore no tax is raised. Special rules mean that banks can often avoid paying stamp duty when they buy and sell property and shares.

Scrap stamp duty

Property and shares should be taxed on an ongoing basis. The reduction in stamp duty as part of the policy response to the Covid-19 epidemic has had a positive impact on the number of house purchases. The proper application of rates, council tax, corporation tax, income tax and capital gains tax should apply to all – including banks! If stamp duty is removed, the free market will be better able to match housing to the needs of families. Scrapping the tax will remove an unfair advantage financial institutions have when transacting property and shares.

INFLATION

The inflation target

The Bank of England is tasked with creating inflation every year. Inflation erodes the value of money – prices rise – and our wages don't always keep up with the cost of living. House prices in the UK have benefited from dramatic inflation over the past fifty years and this has meant more and more of us are left behind.

The cancer eating away at our society

Inflation is a tax on those without assets paid to indebted governments and the wealthy. The rich get a perverse double benefit from inflation – their property values rise, while the real value of the debts they owe falls. Contrast this with people who don't own property but see rents rise and the value of their savings fall. Think about the different impact on the North, Scotland, Wales and Northern Ireland versus the south of England, where much of our wealth is. Inflation is pernicious and it is government policy.

Scrap the inflation target

The Bank of England should be tasked with looking after the integrity of our monetary system – perhaps a target of zero inflation. It certainly should not be the role of the Bank to destroy the value of money. A properly functioning economy will have periods of inflation and also periods of deflation – when things like housing get cheaper – imagine that! Over the years these tend to even out, as happened in Britain in the 19th century.

JAIL IS FOR THE LITTLE PEOPLE

Tax avoidance versus benefit cheat

Our legal system seems to have an inbuilt bias in favour of the wealthy. A person who cheats on their benefits will face the full force of the law. By contrast, the wealthy asset owner who gets out of paying tax seems to get away with it. Benefit fraud is a tiny fraction of the cost of tax evasion.

Irresponsible bankers poisoned our society

Isn't it odd that if you get caught breaking into someone's home and stealing stuff you are likely to go to prison but if you destroy a bank through ignorance and greed and plunge our society into a financial crisis that will take generations to resolve, you walk away?

Our judicial system needs to be reviewed for bias

Our laws and judiciary need to be properly reviewed to reduce bias in favour of the rich. Directors of financial institutions and other companies should face criminal charges for dangerously de-stabilising behaviour. Property is apparently nine tenths of the law, that doesn't mean that wealthy property owners should be able to behave in a way that undermines the basis of trust in our society. The ancient defence against judicial bias is trial by jury. We should consider reversing the decline in the proportion of cases tried this way.

A-ZofInequality.com

KICKING THE CAN DOWN THE ROAD

Growth in government debt

During the pandemic and previously in the financial crisis, the government has grown debt so that it is now more than our GDP – the UK's annual national income. This debt is a burden on our children and grandchildren. Moreover, it means that government has a vested interest in inflating these debts away and therefore increasing the inequality that inflation creates.

The government's hidden debts and other liabilities

The official figures don't include the unfunded state pension liabilities and private finance initiative (PFI) debt schemes to build schools and hospitals. The unfunded deficit on the NHS pension scheme alone increases our national debt by over 25 per cent. Why do we expect future generations to pay for today's healthcare? We can't keep kicking the can down the road.

The government should own up to all of its liabilities

Government should adopt the same accounting principles as companies when recognising what will have to be paid. All UK government liabilities, including pension schemes and PFI, should be recognised in the National Debt figures. If we want to vote in a government who wishes to increase debt – for example to pay for infrastructure or help an economy deal with a recession or a pandemic – that is democracy in action. What is not OK, is for a government to pretend to itself and the rest of us that it is not running up debt for future generations to repay.

LIFETIME ISAS

Tax-free savings

Each year individuals are allowed to save more than many people earn in a year into Lifetime and other Individual Savings Accounts (ISAs). Couples can currently put £40,000 in per year. Once the savings are in these accounts, then any income from interest or dividends or capital gains from the sale of shares is not subject to tax.

Avoiding income and capital gains tax

Families who have been rich enough to save their full entitlement each year into these tax-free schemes, now have millions of pounds' worth of assets that are not subject to income or capital gains tax. These families now earn more in their tax-free savings pots each year than many families earn from working. Earning an income without having to work is an enormous privilege that most people can only dream of. Why is this privilege subsidised by government?

Rebalance taxation to make it fairer for workers

If workers keep subsidising savers, we are heading for resentment between generations and social groups. We must remove the tax breaks for Lifetime and other ISAs. If we tax savings income and capital gains a bit more, we can reduce taxes on work – income tax, employees' NI and employers' NI – and make for a fairer balance.

MARGINAL RATES OF INCOME TAX

High tax rates act as a disincentive to work

Benefits rules mean that when people start working, or increase their working hours, they can end up keeping very little of what they earn. Equally, at the other end of the spectrum, well-paid people often pay high marginal tax rates, in excess of 70 per cent when you take into account employers' NI and the loss of Income Tax Personal Allowances. With the latest increases in employee and employers' NI, some young people are keeping less than half their gross payroll cost.

Work creates wealth and well-being

All wealth is created through work. And work is so important to our well-being. High marginal rates of tax can stop people at all levels of income from working more but are particularly problematic for low earners, graduates and high earners. The most vulnerable and the most productive are being discouraged from helping themselves and contributing to society.

The 50 per cent rule

If you lose more than half your income at source it is a real disincentive to work. Total deductions above the 50 per cent mark (including employers' NI, student loan repayments and loss of benefits) should be adjusted to keep rates below 50 per cent. The recent change to Universal Credit is positive in this regard but still means people only keep 45 pence in the pound. If we start taxing those with assets more, we can put less strain on the working.

A-ZofInequality.com

NATIONAL INSURANCE

Hidden tax on work

National Insurance – recently increased by the Chancellor – is paid by employers, employees and the self-employed. It was originally introduced to help people pay for healthcare, provide old-age pensions and insurance against unemployment. It is now just part of general taxation. People think that the money is being put aside for retirement – but it isn't.

The wealthy often don't pay

Some businesspeople can receive pay in ways that avoid NI, pensioners typically don't pay it and most income from property and shares is exempt. Moreover, people who own assets, such as a large home and garden, often need to employ people to clean, garden and do maintenance. The lower limit for NI is set so these part-time jobs don't require contributions. Working parents and their child carer must pay NI, but the person with a gardener doesn't – funny that.

Combine National Insurance with income tax

National Insurance – whether paid by employees, employers or the self-employed – is really a form of income tax. There is no reason why it is separated out, other than to disguise the amount of tax working people have to pay. NI should be combined with income tax, at lower overall rates, and made applicable to all. This would be simpler and fairer.

OFFSHORE TAX HAVENS

Tax avoidance and tax evasion

Some companies and wealthy individuals hold shares and other assets in countries that cater to the needs of those not wanting to pay their fair share. In some cases, companies pretend that their trading activities and related profits are not taking place in the UK, so that they can avoid paying corporation tax. Whether the use of offshore facilities is tax avoidance (legal) or tax evasion (illegal), it still results in a loss to the UK treasury.

Rules and loopholes

The problem with a tax system that is becoming increasingly based on written rules is that those with the resources to buy smart advice tend to find ways to get round the rules. This puts an unfair burden on ordinary taxpayers who ultimately have to foot the bill. It is extraordinarily irresponsible of both the Blair and Cameron families to have taken advantage of offshore loopholes to get out of tax. If Prime Ministers' families do this, it destroys the basis of trust that our society is built on.

Transparency and a return to the common law / fair play

Sunlight is the best disinfectant. Companies and individuals should be required to state where their assets are held. Complex tax cases should be examined under common law so that the commercial substance of what is happening can be uncovered and a reasonable level of tax agreed.

A-ZofInequality.com

PLANNING REGULATION

Complex systems are an advantage to those with deep pockets

Our planning regulation has become increasingly complex. This tends to favour large corporations and house builders who can employ specialists to help achieve planning. Smaller companies, community schemes and individuals are often disadvantaged by not having the resources to get permission to build.

Where are the homes?

The past twenty years has seen strong population growth in the UK and yet the rate at which we build homes has not really budged. House building is far below the level required. House and apartment building for the less well-off has collapsed for more than a generation. Yet somehow planning restrictions haven't stopped us building luxury homes and offices.

Simplify planning

The planning system needs to be reviewed to reduce the advantage that wealthy corporations have over individual and community schemes. Freeing up planning and other restrictions to enable social and affordable house building is an absolute priority. Land with planning permission that has been unused for over five years should attract council tax.

QUANTITATIVE EASING

Losing trust in our money

Our monetary system is trust based – it requires us all to believe in it. Only 'really clever' people think that printing money – known as quantitative easing (QE) – is a good idea. The rest of us know it is extraordinarily dangerous. If government can conjure money out of thin air it makes a mockery of hard work and saving up. Every school student can make the connection between printing money and the collapse of the economy that happened in Germany after the First World War.

The wealthy benefitted from QE

If money is being printed you want to be standing next to the printer and spend it before everyone else understands what is happening. Who do you think was standing next to the QE printer post the financial crisis and during the pandemic? The City enjoyed a boost in share prices and London property values. The wealthy were protected from deflation – falling asset prices. In fact, the value of their assets grew. The young were denied the chance to buy cheaper housing.

Let's stop passing the pain on to our children

We need to stop printing money and gradually reverse the QE that has happened. It will be painful, but responsible. Housing and other assets will become cheaper. Ultimately, good for the young and others who haven't yet had a chance to buy property.

A-ZofInequality.com

RATES AND COUNCIL TAX

A property tax that is often a tax on work

Rates are due on commercial property and council tax is paid on residential property. The taxes are paid by those who run businesses or live in the property. This means that in many cases the property owner pays nothing, as the tax is paid by the business or residential tenant. In other words, rates and council tax are a further burden on those that work, as opposed to those that own assets. Owner-occupiers do pay these taxes, but owners of expensive houses have the amount they pay capped.

Ownership is a privilege underpinned by our stable society

Earning money from property is a huge privilege; it can only happen in a well-mannered society where property rights are protected by the state. The creation and maintenance of the civic society in the UK did not happen by accident and is not free. It is extraordinary that property owners don't pay their fair share.

Property owners should pay

Property taxes should be paid by the property owner. This would reduce the burden on some of the most productive parts of the economy – businesses and workers who rent. The tax paid should relate to the value of the property so that owners of mansions should pay more than those living in a more modest home.

SELF-INVESTED PERSONAL PENSIONS (SIPPS)

SIPPs

High earners have a choice between paying high rates of tax or paying no tax at all, by putting a substantial amount of money into a personal pension. The government is incentivising people to save for their retirement when these people would save anyway. It seems an odd priority for government subsidy in a country with such a need for housing, healthcare, infrastructure and other priorities, particularly when we have the safety net of a state pension.

Why do we value idleness over work?

It does seem strange that we penalise work through often very high rates of tax and then subsidise not working in the form of generous incentives for pension saving. Work creates the wealth that our whole society benefits from. Retiring and living on a pension is a privilege that does not need to be subsidised.

Tax work a bit less and stop subsidising wealthy retirement

Rates of income tax and National Insurance on work need to be reduced. Retirement savings should then not be subsidised – pension contributions should be made after tax. There is certainly no case for subsiding SIPPs. They are the preserve of the wealthy and can be passed on to children like other assets – in some cases free from inheritance tax.

A-ZofInequality.com

TRUSTS AND INHERITANCE TAX

Voluntary taxes for the 1 per cent

The wealthy use all sorts of mechanisms to limit the tax they pay through the use of trusts. Inheritance tax can be avoided through trusts amongst a myriad of measures. Owners of businesses and land and those who can make gifts in their own lifetime avoid it… but only the really rich can afford to tie up or give away a large proportion of their wealth before they die.

Inheritance tax hurts the non-super rich

Inheritance tax forces many elderly people to make difficult decisions. Should they be moving out of their home? How much money do they need for care? At the same time, the rich use business ownership, farmland and trusts to avoid the tax while continuing to enjoy their wealth.

Tax people while they are alive

If we taxed property, savings and investments properly while people are alive there would be no need for inheritance tax. One idea might be to tax the recipients of inheritance at their income tax rate. Alternatively, it might be simpler to scrap inheritance tax – the really wealthy don't pay it anyway. The beneficiaries of trusts should be taxed like everyone else.

UNPAID WAGES

Low pay and the social safety net

Millions of people in the UK are paid so badly their earnings don't cover the basic needs of food, housing, utilities and other essentials. Benefits – our safety net – have to be used to keep people above the breadline. The safety net is being used to subsidise businesses that pay these poor wages.

A taboo that puts working people at a disadvantage

Why should companies get away with paying low wages? We need to break the ridiculous taboo around what people earn. In some companies it is a disciplinary offence to tell a colleague what you earn. How can such important information for life decisions be a disciplinary matter? Another taboo is the entirely unpaid work of many carers.

How about paying people properly?

Low pay and indeed no pay is best solved through transparency. There is some evidence that minimum wage legislation can have unforeseen adverse consequences; particularly for the most disadvantaged. Nonetheless, the living wage concept is an excellent start. Companies that pay people so badly that they cannot afford to live should be named and shamed and social media is enabling this. Shame is a powerful motivator; as is customers deciding not to use a business that doesn't treat its people properly. Employees moving to an organisation that values them is the most powerful agent of change of all.

VAT

VAT was originally designed to be a tax on luxuries

VAT of 20 per cent is currently levied on most consumer goods – many of which are by no means luxuries. This consumer tax disproportionately impacts those who are less well off because a much higher proportion of their income is spent on goods and services that attract VAT. And VAT tends to dampen economic activity.

Those with assets enjoy them VAT free

For most people a day out, a holiday or enjoying a hobby means paying quite a lot of VAT. A strange side effect of being wealthy is that much of your leisure time can be enjoyed VAT free. Indeed, the ownership of assets such as farmland and holiday homes is subsidised by numerous government policies. It is extraordinary that the person on the camping holiday pays VAT but the owner of the holiday home doesn't. What could be more of a luxury than owning a second home in a country where many young families can't even rent a home?

Levy VAT with care and level the playing field

VAT is a regressive tax (it impacts the less well-off more), so there may well be a case for reducing the rate. It is to the credit of the UK that much of our countryside and coast can be enjoyed by all. Holiday homes should either be subject to VAT, as other holidays are, or have double council tax.

WOMEN AND WEALTH

Marriage is for the rich

Women typically hold less wealth than men and so are at an inherent disadvantage in a society that protects and subsidises wealth. Moreover, the wealthy are able to minimise tax through having a partner, whereas permanent relationships penalise those on low incomes.

Unforeseen consequences in family life

The image of the wealthy wife – on the yacht in the Mediterranean – paying no income tax, is in sharp contrast with the single mum who loses her benefits if she moves in with her partner. Wealthy couples pretend to live together in order to continue to reduce their current and future tax bills. Poorer couples pretend to live apart in order to protect their benefits. Poorer couples are incentivised by the state to split up their families in order to protect their income.

Taxation and subsidies should relate to individuals

It is not the role of the state to start incentivising and penalising different types of family life. Taxation and benefits policies should relate to individuals. If benefits are needed, these should be paid regardless of marital and civil partnership status. Equally, the wealthy should not be able to use marriage as a form of tax avoidance.

X MARKS THE SPOT OF HIDDEN TREASURE

The homes no one lives in

The UK has a real shortage of housing. The rate of building new homes has fallen behind the pace at which we are forming new households for over ten years. We are perhaps over a million homes short – a shortage that is particularly acute in London. Despite this, much of what we have built in the past ten years in London is apartment blocks that nobody lives in.

Bullion bars in the sky

The apartments in these well-appointed glass towers are often sold to overseas buyers looking to store some wealth in the safe haven that is the UK. These are the bullion bars in the sky. They are sometimes used for a couple of weeks a year for a London holiday, but ordinary people are not even given the opportunity to rent these properties.

Double council tax

Planning permission for housing is of huge value in a peaceful and law-abiding society. It is extraordinary that there is apparently no shame in keeping property empty in a city with homelessness and where families are being relocated to housing in other parts of the country. Owners who keep properties empty for much of the year should perhaps pay double council tax.

A-Z of Inequality.com

YOUNG PEOPLE

Shouldering the nation's debts

In the ten years following the financial crisis the UK government tripled the national debt. The level of official debt now exceeds the total amount earned by all of us in the UK in a year. The unofficial level is much higher. This level of debt means there will be less spending available in the future. The younger generations will have to go without – not just now – but for decades.

Having a mortgage without owning a home

At the same time that young people had the tripling of the national debt imposed on them, the Conservative and Liberal Democrat coalition decided to triple the tuition fees introduced by Labour. There are protections for the low paid and, as with so much else, it won't impact the very wealthy. For most people the scheme appears to have an incredibly high interest rate and repayments act like an additional 9 per cent income tax.

Improve student loan terms and consider an amnesty

There needs to be an immediate reduction on both the interest paid on student loans and the rate at which they are repaid. There may be grounds for an amnesty for some students. Education has always been a precious gift from the old to the young; let's make it so again.

ZERO INTEREST RATE POLICY (ZIRP)

Governments want to create inflation

The Bank of England currently aims to keep the base interest rate close to zero in order to meet its inflation target. Low base rates are intended to stimulate borrowing. There is even talk of negative base rates. This makes it easier for the UK government to rack up debt that future generations will have to repay.

ZIRP helps the rich but not the poor

This policy affects the rich and poor very differently. Rich companies and individuals can borrow money cheaply against their assets. Most people have to pay much higher rates of interest on mortgages, overdrafts and credit cards. Payday lenders don't operate ZIRP. Poorer families have a higher proportion of wealth in savings and suffer low interest income.

End interest rate setting by the Bank of England

If you manipulate a market it leads to the misallocation of resources. There are millions of transactions a year involving borrowing and lending; plenty enough for markets to be able to set interest rates. Unelected officials at the Bank of England should not have a mandate to interfere with a market by setting artificially low interest rates. The Bank of England should be tasked with the long-term stability of our monetary system and this is better achieved through prudent oversight of financial institutions.

CONCLUSION

One of the striking things about many of the state causes of inequality is how straightforward they would be to reverse. In a lot of cases, it just means changing a minor piece of legislation; no more difficult than the sort of changes typically made in the Chancellor's budget.

Do we really need Lifetime ISAs? These enable rich families to move millions of assets outside of the clutches of income tax, National Insurance and capital gains tax. And what about SIPPs? Incentivising high earners to save for a pension can't be a priority for a cash-strapped government. The capital gains tax allowance is equally ridiculous; it is set at a level similar to the income tax free allowance and helps the poor folk that make substantial gains on assets (of course, not including the large homes, pensions and ISAs – which are CGT exempt). There is no case for subsidising land ownership, second homes and offshore arrangements.

If work was not so heavily taxed, then the need for things like tax breaks on pension contributions and subsidies for the lower paid would reduce. The formula is simple. Wealth is created by work. Heavy taxes reduce work. We need wealth to pay for a decent society.

Removing some of the rules that only those with substantial wealth can take advantage of would make a start of simplifying our tax code. Editing down the existing tax code would indeed be a difficult task. The easier approach would be to start afresh. Written from first principles in language that can be understood and with supporting illustrations of how a tax is expected to operate is not an impossible task. Fewer rules means fewer loopholes and more room for a Common Law / common sense approach to tax compliance.

Stopping companies from deducting interest costs from their taxable profits has widespread support from economists. Interest rates are at their lowest levels in recorded history. Any company that can't afford to do this must be barely solvent. It has to be an optimal time to make this change. The positive consequences, from levelling the playing field to stabilising our monetary system, are immeasurable.

What of the monetary system? How difficult would it be stop pulling the cancerous apples from the magic money tree? Quantitative Easing did not really exist prior to the financial crisis. Massive government debt has been tackled before – in the aftermath of the Second World War. Further back, we managed to get through the 19th and early 20th centuries without creating inflation and manipulating interest rates. Talking about the real level of government liabilities is up to us, not government.

We can do this.

There is a stark choice. We either make these simple changes to reduce the government sponsorship of inequality or we stay on track to create a polarised, poorer and less stable society.

I am optimistic. The UK has a long history of making difficult changes to steer us away from disaster. We just need to:

- Stop subsidising wealth
- Tax work less
- Make the rules simpler and fairer
- Stop corrupting our monetary system
- Stop running up hidden debts for the next generation to pay.

Let's work together with young people, to make these changes happen.

ACKNOWLEDGEMENTS

Much thanks to all who have supported this project over the years, particularly Helena Maxwell and Laurens McDonald. I am indebted to the comments of those who read the first draft – Charlie Jacoby, Harry Bott, Hattie Ghaui, Jane Butcher and Karen Howes. I have been much influenced by the MoneyWeek team – all thanks to Bill Boner, Dominic Frisby, Merryn Somerset Webb and John Stepek. Amelia Collins at whitefox has been so patient at guiding me; as has Katie Butcher who has got me into social media. Finally, all thanks to Rob Shreeve, my agent, whose support has been expert, relentless and fun.

Published in 2022 by Sebastian Chambers
In partnership with whitefox publishing

Copyright © Sebastian Chambers, 2022
Illustrations © Helena Maxwell, 2022

The right of Sebastian Chambers to be identified as the author of this work has been asserted in accordance with Section 77 of the Copyright, Designs and Patents Act 1988.

All rights reserved. No part of this publication may be reproduced, stored in a retrieval system, or transmitted in any form or by any means, electronic, mechanical, photocopying, recording or otherwise, without prior written permission of the author.

ISBN 978-1-915036-01-8

Designed by Jonathan Baker, Seagull Design
Cover designed by Madeline Meckiffe
Project management by whitefox
Printed and bound in the UK by CPI